A PET OR NOT?

ALVIN SILVERSTEIN · VIRGINIA SILVERSTEIN · LAURA SILVERSTEIN NUNN

TWENTY-FIRST CENTURY BOOKS
BROOKFIELD, CONNECTICUT

Cover photograph courtesy of Animals, Animals (© Robert Pearcy)

Photographs courtesy of Animals, Animals: pp. 6 (© Ken Cole), 14 (© Reed Williams), 22 (© Barbara Wright), 26 (© Barbara Wright), 30 (© Ken Cole), 34 (© Zig Leszczynski); Visuals Unlimited: pp. 10 (© 1996 Milton H. Tierney, Jr.), 38 (© Scott Berner); Photo Researchers, Inc.: pp. 18 (© Hans Reinhard/OKAPIA), 42 (© Alan & Sandy Carey)

Cover Design by Karen Quigley
Interior Design by Claire Fontaine

Library of Congress Cataloging–in–Publication Data

Silverstein, Alvin.
A pet or not? / Alvin Silverstein, Virginia Silverstein, Laura Silverstein Nunn.
p. cm. — (What a Pet!)
Includes bibliographical references (p.) and index.
Summary: Discusses the pros and cons of owning exotic pets such as armadillos, llamas, monkeys, potbellied pigs, and sugar gliders, and offers advice on their care, feeding, and emotional support.
ISBN 0-7613-3230-8 (lib. bdg.)
1. Pets—Juvenile literature. 2. Wild animals as pets—Juvenile literature. [1. Wild animals as pets. 2. Pets.]
I. Silverstein, Virginia B. II. Nunn, Laura Silverstein. III. Title. IV. Series: Silverstein, Alvin. What a Pet!
SF416.2.S55 1999
636.088'7—dc21
98-46358
CIP AC

Published by Twenty-First Century Books
A Division of The Millbrook Press, Inc.
2 Old New Milford Road
Brookfield, Connecticut 06804

CONTENTS

WHAT A PET!

THIS SERIES WILL GIVE you information about some well-known animals and some unusual ones. It will help you to select a pet suitable for your family and for where you live. It will also tell you about animals that should *not* be pets. It is important for you to understand that many people who work with animals are strongly opposed to keeping *any* wild creature as a pet.

People tend to want to keep exotic animals. But they forget that often it is illegal to have them as pets, or that they require a great deal of special care and will never really become good pets. A current fad of owning an exotic animal may quickly pass, and the animals suffer. Their owners may abandon them in an effort to return them to the wild, even though the animals can no longer survive there. Or they may languish in small cages without proper food and exercise.

Before selecting any animal as a pet, it is a good idea to learn as much as you can about it. This series will help you, and your local veterinarian and the ASPCA are good sources of information. You should also find out if it is endangered. Phone numbers for each state wildlife agency can be found on the Internet at

http://www.animalsforsale.com/states.htm

and you can get an updated list of endangered and threatened species on the Internet at

http://jjwww.fws.gov/r9endspp/endspp.html "Endangered Species Home Page, U.S. Fish & Wildlife Service"

Any pet is a big responsibility—*your* responsibility. The most important thing to keep in mind when selecting a pet is the welfare of the animal.

FAST FACTS

Scientific name	*Dasypus novemcinctus* in Family Dasypodidae, Order Edentata
Cost	Hard to get unless you live in a southern state where you can live-trap them
Food	Canned dog food, cooked egg, insects
Housing	A strong cage indoors and (in warm localities) an outdoor pen with a fence reinforced against digging
Training	Can be housebroken; not very smart at learning tricks
Special notes	Some places require a special permit to keep armadillos.

ARMADILLO

ARMADILLO

WHAT PET COULD BE MORE unusual than an animal in armor? Armadillos are one of only two mammals with a suit of armor, like an old-time knight. Actually, that is how they got their name—*armadillo* means "little armored one" in Spanish. The armadillo's hard shell is made up of small plates of bone, fitted closely together. Movable bands of tough skin around its back give it some flexibility. Patches of coarse hair grow between the armor plates.

ANCIENT HISTORY

Armadillos belong to a very ancient group of mammals, which also includes anteaters and sloths. The name of the group, Edentata, literally means "toothless." Anteaters really are toothless, but armadillos have a few peg-shaped back teeth. Like their relatives, they eat mainly insects and grubs, which they slurp up with flicks of a long, sticky tongue.

There are twenty different species (kinds) of armadillos. Most of them live in South America. Only one species can be found in the United States: the nine-banded armadillo, named for the number of bands on its armor.

A LONG JOURNEY

Armadillos first appeared on Earth about 50 million years ago in South America. About 2.5 million years ago, a land bridge formed between the North American and South American continents. Some armadillos, including one species as large as a black bear, traveled up into what is now the United States and settled there. Then, about five to ten thousand years ago, they all died out except for some nine-banded armadillos in what is now Mexico.

During the nineteenth century, this armadillo species began an amazing comeback. By about 1850 nine-banded armadillos were spotted in southern Texas. Deserts blocked them from moving westward, but they soon spread to the north and east. Rivers and streams did not block their way. Armadillos are good swimmers, dog paddling or floating in the water. (They gulp in air to make themselves lighter.) They can also cross small rivers or streams by walking on the bottom, holding their breath for as long as six minutes.

By the 1940s armadillos had crossed the Mississippi River, perhaps by floating on driftwood or hitching rides on boats. By the 1970s some had reached the Florida panhandle. Florida already had another growing population of nine-banded armadillos, descended from a few animals that had escaped from captivity near Cocoa, Florida, half a century before. Today, an estimated 30 to 50 million nine-banded armadillos live in the United States—in Texas, Alabama, southern Oklahoma, Kansas, Arkansas, Mississippi, Louisiana, and Florida.

LIVING IN ARMOR

A nine-banded armadillo is about the size of a cat, with a body 15 to 17 inches (38 to 43 centimeters) long and a tail that is 14 to 16 inches (36 to 41 centimeters) long. It weighs 8 to 17 pounds (3.6 to 7.7 kilograms).

Armadillos are nocturnal animals—that is, they are active at night and rest during the day. They use their long, sticky, wormlike tongues to feast on ants, grubs (insect larvae), spiders, worms, snakes, lizards, snails, and sometimes dead animals. They use their large, powerful front claws to dig deep into anthills or to dig burrows to rest in.

Digging also comes in handy when danger threatens. An armadillo can dig a shallow burrow very quickly. It then tucks in its head and feet. Luckily for the armadillo, most predators cannot get past its tough armor shell. Armadillos do not always succeed when they try to escape danger, however. In Texas and Florida they often wind up as roadkill, mainly because of their unfortunate habit of jumping straight up into the air when they are scared. As a result, many are killed by cars. (If they did not move, cars might pass over them without harm.)

> **DID YOU KNOW?**
> An armadillo's long, sticky tongue can scoop up 60 to 70 insects in one lick!

Armadillos are strictly warm-weather animals. Unlike most mammals, they do not use much energy to produce heat, and their legs can get chilled very easily if the weather is too cool. They also do not store fat for food reserves, so they must find food to eat every day. These are the main reasons they have not moved into the northern states.

ARMADILLO PETS

Armadillos can make interesting pets, but they take a lot of hard work. After they get used to humans, they do not mind being handled. (Wild armadillos don't bite but may give nasty scratches.) They do not shed hair or dander (flakes of skin) that might bother people with allergies. Armadillos can also be trained to use a litter box, although they have a rather smelly body odor. Since these animals are naturally nocturnal, they tend to be active at night, making lots of noise when you would rather be sleeping. (They do not seem to mind being awakened to play during the day, though.)

Some people regard armadillos as pests because they dig up gardens. If they are allowed to run free outdoors, they can make a big mess out of your yard—and the neighbors' yards, too, if your fence is not armadillo-proof. (Remember, they are great diggers.)

> ### DID YOU KNOW?
> Nine-banded armadillos always give birth to a litter of four identical quadruplets. The babies are born with soft shells, which get harder as they grow.

> ### *Cyberdillo*
> *If you do not want to take care of a real live armadillo, you can adopt a cyberdillo! Pick out your "virtual" armadillo pet on the Internet at* **http:www.cyber-ramp.net/~dmorgan/pickapet.html**

A more serious problem is that some wild armadillos may carry leprosy, a disease that is devastating to humans. This is the main reason Texas does not permit armadillos to be shipped out of the state, unless they are to be used for research on this disease. So if you want to keep an armadillo pet, have it tested by a veterinarian first!

INTERNET RESOURCES

http://pandoras-box.org/my05026.htm Eleanor E. Storrs, "The Astonishing Armadillo," *National Geographic* article by an armadillo researcher.

http://pilot.msu.edu/user/nixonjos/index.htm/main.htm "Armadillo Online" (armadillo information, pictures, links)

http://www.armadilloent.com/pettrk.html "Armadillo Pet Tricks" (animations to download and a dillo fan club; not for real, but fun)

http://www.cyberramp.net/~dmorgan/ "Cyberdillo" (armadillo fun, links)

http://www.kiva.net/~drdillo/dillogif.htm "Armadillo GIFs and JPEGs" (pictures of armadillos)

COATIMUNDI

FAST FACTS

Scientific name	*Nasua nasua* in Family Procyonidae, Order Carnivora
Cost	$650 to $1000
Food	Beef dog food, insects, mealworms, crickets, fruits, vegetables, nuts, cooked egg
Housing	Large, tall wire cage, at least 6-by-6-by-6 feet (2-by-2-by-2 meters), must include a sturdy tree branch for climbing. Put a strong lock on the door. Coatis can undo any latch eventually. Include plenty of toys to avoid boredom.
Training	Be gentle and use positive rewards, not punishment. Can be trained to wear a leash. Can also be trained to use a litter box. Can learn to be a part of the family.
Special notes	It may be illegal to own a coatimundi in some areas, or a permit may be needed.

COATIMUNDI

IMAGINE A PET THAT IS affectionate and loving, and very enjoyable to watch. But at the same time, it is extremely curious and mischievous, with "trouble" as its middle name. That sounds like a coatimundi. Coatis are fun-loving creatures, but they sure can be a handful.

LITTLE RASCALS

Coatimundis, or coatis, belong to the raccoon family. Like their raccoon relatives, coatis look like masked bandits. In this case, looks are not deceiving. Coatis are little rascals. These mischievous creatures are very smart and very curious, and they are great with their "hands." They can open almost any drawer or cabinet and make a big mess of their owner's home. Coatis are very active animals and get bored easily. So they need plenty of toys to keep them busy. Needless to say, coati-proofing the house is a must.

A COATIMUNDI'S LIFE

Several species of coatimundis live in South America, Central America, and Mexico. In the 1900s one species, the white-nosed coati, moved up into the United States as well, settling in Texas, Arizona, and New Mexico. Coatis adapt very well to different types of environments, from jungle to desert, but they do need a warm climate. If the temperature drops below 40°F (about 4°C), a coatimundi's tail may get frostbitten and fall off!

The coatimundi's body is 16 to 26 inches (about 40 to 50 centimeters) long with a tail that is about the same length. It weighs 6.5 to 13 pounds (3 to 6 kilograms). Males are larger than the females. The coati's coat may be black to reddish brown, with off-white or creamy yellow on the underparts of the body. It has dark feet and a ringed tail. The coati has a distinct face mask and a long, flexible snout to poke around rocks and crevices in search of insects and other favorite foods. The coati's nose is very sensitive and can sniff out food underground. It then uses its strong claws to dig it out.

In the wild, female coatis are very social animals. They live together in groups of six to twenty females and their offspring. The females protect each other, groom each other, and help raise each other's young. Male coatis, on the other hand, live alone, except during mating season. In fact, *coatimundi* is an Indian word meaning "lone coati." Adult males may also hunt at night, even though the species is mainly diurnal (active during the day). Biologists originally thought that the males and females belonged to two different species because their habits were so different.

COATIMUNDI PETS

Coatimundis can make very interesting pets. They are fun and very affectionate and do not mind being held by humans. Like other animals, coatis become tame and gentle when they are given plenty of attention, especially when they are young. Still, coatimundis are curious by nature and are likely to get into trouble. So when your pet coati has free run of your home, keep an eye on it. Coatis are excellent climbers and are often found in trees in the wild, so a coati house pet will probably climb all over the furniture. Coatis also tend to jump from place to place, and that may include you. Their sharp claws can really hurt when they land on your shoulders or your legs. Some people recommend declawing the coati, but other people say the best thing to do is to teach the coati at a very young age not to jump on people.

Coatis can be trained to wear a collar and walk on a leash. They can also be taught to use a litter box. Like all pets, coatis should be treated gently but firmly.

Raising a coatimundi is a lot of hard work and may not be for everyone. (It is definitely not a good pet choice for young children.) With a life span of 14 years, a pet coati also requires a big commitment. Its owner

DID YOU KNOW?

The coati is the only member of the raccoon family that is diurnal, or active during the day. The other family members are active at night (nocturnal), except for the panda, which is active at dawn and dusk (crepuscular).

should be dedicated, loving, and especially patient to have a happy and loving relationship with this remarkable animal.

INTERNET RESOURCES

http://planetpets.simplenet.com/plntcoti.htm "Planet Coati" (pictures and information)

http://www.animalsforsale.com/coatimundi.htm "Coatimundi" by Pat Storey (background, photos, and pet tips at the R-Zu-2-U Web site)

http://www.belizenet.com/zoo/zoo/mammals/coa/coa1.html "Coatimundi" (background information on coatis in Belize, with photos, a video of a coati in its habitat, and coati sounds)

http://www.blarg.net/~critter/articles/sm_furry/mundi1.html "Coatimundi Care Sheet" by Tom Columbano (good information on coati pet care)

http://www.blarg.net/~critter/articles/sm_furry/mundi2.html "Commonly Asked Questions About the Coatimundi" by Tom Columbano

http://www.blarg.net/~critter/articles/sm_furry/mundi3.html "Coatimundi (*Nasua nasua*)" by Linda Watkins (more pet care information)

http://www.desertusa.com/may97/du_coati2.html "White-Nosed Coati (Coatimundi)" (background information and pictures)

FAST FACTS

Scientific name	*Mustela furo* in Family Mustelidae
Cost	$75 to $250; average price $150.
Food	Ferret food, premium cat food. Use water bottle and nontip food dish.
Housing	Wire cage must include three important areas: a tissue box for sleeping, a litter box area, a place to eat. Put ferret in a kiddie pool in the summer to cool off.
Training	Use positive rewards (not punishment) to teach commands, tricks, and litter box training; treat ferrets gently.
Special notes	It is illegal to own ferrets in some areas. Some other places require a permit or license to have a pet ferret.

FERRET

FERRET

WOULD YOU LIKE A PET as playful as a cat and as intelligent as a dog? How about a pet ferret? Ferrets are very smart, fun-loving animals, but they are also very curious, which can get them into a lot of trouble.

FUN AND GAMES

Ferrets love to explore. If you let your ferret roam freely through the house, keep an eye on it. You will see just how much trouble this cute little critter can get into. Experienced ferret owners know that before you bring home a ferret, you need to "ferret-proof" your house. That is, make sure your ferret cannot get into anything that it is not supposed to. Ferrets are well-known escape artists. They can squeeze through the tiniest spaces—between furniture or small gaps in their cage. These crafty critters can even open cupboards and drawers. Ferret-proofing is very important because it's no longer fun if your pet ferret gets hurt.

TRULY DOMESTICATED

People often mistake ferrets for wild animals. The truth is, today's ferrets would not be able to survive in the wild. These animals have been domesticated for over 3,000 years. They were first tamed by the Egyptians, even before the cat. Ferrets were also used by the ancient Romans as work animals to crawl into burrows and chase out the rabbits, mice, and rats that were eating crops.

Domesticated ferrets were first brought from Europe to the United States in the 1870s. They were used for rodent control and were very effective in getting rid of rats and mice. Breeding ferrets became so popular in New London, Ohio, that it became known as Ferretville, USA. However, the ferrets had an appetite for chickens as well. Soon farmers considered ferrets to be worse pests than the rodents. As a result, some places made pet ferrets illegal. Since the 1970s, though, ferrets have been gaining popularity as pets. In fact, now there are veterinarians who specialize in ferrets.

> **JUST A SUGGESTION**
> Put a lightweight collar with a bell on your ferret's neck so you can keep track of your pet and keep it out of trouble.

A FERRET'S LIFE

Ferrets belong to the weasel family, which includes the weasel, mink, otter, sable, badger, and skunk. The domestic ferret is sometimes confused with its distant cousin, the black-footed ferret, which is endangered in the United States. Though these animals look similar, they are probably not very closely related. The domestic ferret's closest relatives are actually the European polecat and the steppe polecat found in Siberia.

Domestic ferrets have a long slender body about 14 to 16 inches (36 to 41 centimeters) long, and weigh about 2 to 5 pounds (0.9 to 2.3 kilograms). Females are smaller than males. Ferrets come in a variety of colors. Sable, marked with a raccoonlike mask, is the most popular. Other colors include butterscotch, cinnamon, albino, and sterling silver.

Ferrets are very sociable animals and communicate with sounds and body language. They hop and bounce to show excitement. Ferrets may cluck when they are happy—or when they are angry. A scared ferret will make puffing sounds and arch its back, while its hairs stand straight up, just like a frightened cat. Hissing is also a sign of fear, but screaming means the ferret is in pain.

DID YOU KNOW?
Ferrets cannot handle hot weather and may become ill. Watch out for temperatures greater than 90°F (32°C). Make sure your ferret gets plenty of shade in the summer.

FERRET PETS

Ferrets' sociability and playfulness make them good pets. They like to be in pairs, but they can amuse themselves when they are alone. Ferrets are very playful animals throughout their entire lifetime of 8 to 10 years. They have a variety of games they play with each other and their owners. For instance, some favorite games include tag, hide-and-seek, peek-a-boo, tug-of-war, and mock combat. In mock combat, ferrets often play a little rough and they may also nip a lot. If a game with your pet ferret starts getting out of hand, it is time to stop.

Some Smelly Relatives

Like other members of the weasel family, most notably the skunk, the ferret has scent glands underneath its tail. When frightened, a ferret will spray out a very stinky, musky smell. Fortunately, unlike the skunk, the smell does not last very long. The ferret's musky odor can be reduced by spaying or neutering, as well as descenting the animal. Even after this, the musky smell will not go away completely. The best thing to do is bathe the ferret every week or two.

Ferrets are very smart. They can learn simple commands and even do some tricks, for example, "sit up." You can teach your ferret the word *no*, which can be very useful, especially if it tries to nip you during rough play or gets into something that it is not supposed to. Ferrets can learn how to walk on a leash and to ride on your shoulder. They can also be trained to use the litter box—at least, most of the time.

Treats are very important in training ferrets. The vitamin supplements Linatone and Ferretone make good rewards, not only nutritious but tasty, too. Bitter Apple spray tastes yucky to ferrets and will help keep them from chewing on furniture and other household items. Always be gentle with pet ferrets—they may become aggressive if they are punished harshly.

Ferrets are naturally nocturnal, active mainly at night, but they can learn to adjust their schedule to fit that of their owners.

Ferret owners say that having a pet ferret can be summarized in six descriptive words that spell out the word *ferret*: Fun-loving, Energetic, Rambunctious, Rewarding, Endearing, Trainable.

DID YOU KNOW?
Ferrets are one of the few animals that can catch the flu, just like people. In fact, they can catch the flu from people, and people can catch the flu from a ferret.

INTERNET RESOURCES

http://planetpets.simplenet.com/ferret.htm "Ferrets" (ferret history and pet care tips; link for subscribing to the Independent Ferret News Service)

http://www.ferretcentral.org/faq/part1.html#what_are "Ferret FAQ," by Pam Greene (chock full of useful information on ferret history and every aspect of ferret care; links to mailing lists, online chats, ferret pictures, and how to start a ferret club)

http://www.smu.edu/~hmccowen/ferret.html "What are Ferrets?"

http://www.smu.edu/~hmccowen/f_top_ten.html "Top Ten List of Human Misconceptions about Ferrets," by Nathan Viles (ferret information and links)

FAST FACTS

Scientific name	*Atelerix albiventris* in Family Erinaceidae (Hedgehogs)
Cost	$20 to $35 each from a breeder, but air freight and other charges can run close to $150
Food	Dog or cat food, hedgehog food, eggs, fruit (apple, bananas, raisins), mealworms. Use a water bottle or nontip dish.
Housing	20- or 30-gallon aquarium, a rabbit cage, or similar housing with a protective roof on top; should include bedding with a layer of newspapers and old rags and towels
Training	Can be "litter trained." However, some hedgehogs will just use the litter pan to play.
Special notes	Illegal in some areas

HEDGEHOG

HEDGEHOG

HOW WOULD YOU LIKE a pet that is covered with prickly hairs and looks like a walking pincushion? A hedgehog may not be soft and cuddly like a kitten or obedient like a dog, but pet owners say that hedgehogs are adorable and make fun pets.

A PAINFUL GREETING

The hedgehogs in Lewis Carroll's *Alice in Wonderland* rolled themselves up and were used as the balls in a game of croquet. That's not a very nice thing to do to any animal, but real hedgehogs can roll themselves up into round balls. This is actually their means of defense.

A hedgehog has a prickly coat. Much of its body is covered with spines, which are hollow, pointed hairs up to 1 inch (2.5 centimeters) long. The hedgehog's face, legs, and belly are covered with soft fur. If a hedgehog gets nervous or stressed, it curls its body into a little ball, and the spines stand straight out in all directions. (This is similar to a cat's hair standing up when it gets scared.) When the hedgehog does this, its spines become sharp and too painful to touch, so many predators do not bother with it.

> **DID YOU KNOW?**
> A hedgehog may have up to 5,000 spines on its body.

If you take home a new hedgehog pet, the hedgehog may act frightened of you. It is a good idea to wear gloves at first. After a while, your new pet will get to know your smell. As soon as it becomes relaxed, its spines will flatten down against its body, and its greeting will not be so painful.

HEDGEHOGS AS PETS

Hedgehogs are not native to North America. Various species can be found in the wild in Africa, Europe, and Asia. The hedgehog pet of choice is the African pygmy hedgehog. These animals were not brought to North America until the 1980s. At first they were displayed only in private collections and zoos. Soon, however, raising hedgehogs in captivity became popular, and it became obvious that these little animals would make great pets.

Interest in hedgehogs in North America grew in 1993 when a comic strip called "Hazel the Hedgehog" was created. Later that year, for the first time, commercial hedgehog food became available. Also, a year or so earlier, children could watch a new cartoon show called *Sonic the Hedgehog* on television. ("Sonic the Hedgehog" became a popular video game, as well.) It did not take long before the hedgehog became a household name.

Although African pygmy hedgehogs can no longer be imported, people can get pet hedgehogs from an estimated 2,000 breeding animals that are raised in the United States.

THE LIFE OF A HEDGEHOG

Hedgehogs are small animals; they grow to about 6 to 8 inches (15 to 20 centimeters) long and weigh about a pound (0.45 kilogram). The African pygmy hedgehog comes in a variety of colors that include white, black, cream, and snowflake. But many hedgehogs have a kind of "salt and pepper" look to them. These prickly creatures make puffing and sniffing sounds when they are threatened, disturbed, or irritated. Hedgehogs that are frightened or that are in serious pain let out loud screaming sounds. Happy hedgehogs make soft whistling sounds.

Hedgehogs are very active animals, so they need to have plenty of room in their cages. Exercise wheels are great for keeping them busy. Some people let pet hedgehogs play in their gardens. In fact, the hedgehogs are actually doing them a favor—these animals love to eat insects. But if your hedgehog is allowed to roam freely, keep an eye on it or you may have trouble finding it. Hedgehogs dig burrows, so make sure it does not sneak out under your fence.

In the wild, hedgehogs sleep during most of the day and are active at night. But you can probably turn your pet hedgehog into a "day animal" if you feed it at certain times. Hedgehogs in the wild are also hibernating animals. They need to live in warm temperatures ranging from 65 to 80°F (18 to 27°C). If the tem-

Strange Behavior

If you see your hedgehog foaming at the mouth, do not be alarmed—it does not have rabies. If the hedgehog encounters an unfamiliar smell, it licks the strange substance, which causes large amounts of foaming saliva to form. The hedgehog then twists its body, and uses its long tongue to cover its spines with the saliva. The reason for this strange behavior, called self-anointing, is still a mystery.

Some experts believe that it is a form of defense. Hedgehogs are not affected by most poisons, so when they encounter something toxic, they eat it, foam up, then cover themselves with this toxic mixture. This keeps enemies from bothering them. The substance does not have to be toxic for the hedgehog to foam. Some hedgehogs will foam up if you pick them up after washing your hands, or if your hands are sweaty. Some hedgehogs may not foam up at all.

perature drops below this range, the hedgehog will go into hibernation and you won't be able to wake it up. So make sure your pet hedgehog lives in comfortable temperatures so it can stay active all year round.

Hedgehogs by nature are solitary animals. So it is probably not a good idea to keep more than one in a cage, or they will fight. Hedgehogs can become very affectionate with people when they are handled frequently starting at a young age. A hedgehog may ask for attention by standing upright as it leans against your leg. Or when it wants to go outside, it may scratch on the outside door. It may also make loud screeching sounds to let you know it is hungry.

Hedgehogs are very clean animals. They may need a bath only once or twice a year. Some people are able to train their hedgehog to use a litter box. (It is important to use dust-free, non-clumping kitty litter.) This does not work for all hedgehogs. However, they will often leave droppings roughly in the same area, which makes clean-up a lot easier.

INTERNET RESOURCES

http://fohnix.metronet.com/~mcgary/hedgehogs.html "Hedgehogs," by Mike McGary (information and links to hedgehog pages, pictures, and a game)

http://members.aol.com/hkeane/webdoc2.htm "About Hedgehogs," by Ron Keane (background information, pet care, behavior, and medical concerns)

http://planetpets.simplenet.com/hedgehog.htm "Hedgehogs" (information)

http://www.advantage.ca/~mainse/care.htm "Fairview Hedgehogs: Easy Care!" (information and pictures)

http://www.xmission.com/~hedgehog/hedgehog/faq/ "Hedgehog FAQ" (lots of information on pet care from Hedgehog Central)

F A S T F A C T S

Scientific name	*Lama glama* in Family Camelidae (Camel Family). The alpaca is *Lama pacos*.
Cost	From $100 for a pet, packer, or guard llama up to $4,000 for a breeding female. Alpacas can cost more than $20,000.
Food	Pasture grass, grain, and hay. Unlike other livestock, llamas do not need high-protein and high-energy diets.
Housing	Fenced-in grassy area. A barn or other shelter should be available to protect against extreme temperatures.
Training	Use positive rewards (not punishment) to halter-train or to teach simple commands.
Special notes	Some places may not permit keeping "farm animals."

L L A M A

LLAMAS

MANY PEOPLE THINK that all llamas are wild animals. That is not true. In fact, llamas were domesticated in South America over 5,000 years ago. It was not until the 1980s, however, that llamas started to become popular pets in North America. Many llama owners say that llamas are gentle, intelligent animals that are inexpensive and easy to care for.

Llamas belong to the camel family, but do not have the camel's typical hump. Like their camel relatives, llamas have gotten a bad reputation for something they do—spit. Llamas *do* spit, shooting out a smelly green glob of already digested food that can travel 10 to 15 feet (3 to 4.5 meters). They spit when they are annoyed, or to show dominance; but they usually spit only at other llamas and only rarely at people. Just make sure not to get in the middle of a "food fight" between llamas!

A LONG HISTORY

About three million years ago, ancestors of today's llamas lived in North America and gradually traveled down to South America. Llamas later died out in North America, but about 5,000 years ago the ancient Incas of the Andes Mountains of South America domesticated the llama and its close relative, the alpaca. Through selective breeding, the Incas produced sturdy animals that could carry heavy loads for many miles. These animals were also valued for their wool, which was made into clothing, rugs, ropes, and other items.

Llamas were reintroduced into North America in the 1870s, but for years they could be found only in zoos and private collections. In 1982 there were just over 3,200 llamas in the United States, then their popularity exploded. By the late 1990s there were more than 75,000 llamas in the United States and Canada.

LLAMAS AS PETS

Adult llamas range in weight from 250 to 450 pounds (113 to 204 kilograms). They stand tall—up to 5 to 6 feet (close to 2 meters) at the head. Llamas come in a variety of colors, including white, black, brown, gray, or a mixture of these colors. Llama wool is much softer and warmer than sheep wool.

Llamas are very sociable animals. In the wild, they live in groups. Compared to other large animals, llamas are rather quiet. They communicate by making humming sounds. They use different types of humming sounds to show they are tired, uncomfortable, curious, or hot. Llamas also cluck, "orgle" (a sort of gargling sound), and make loud, high-pitched alarm calls.

Llamas have an expressive body language, too. For instance, a llama will flatten its ears against the sides of its head when it is angry—beware of possible spitting. Ears that are pointed toward the back of the head but not flattened mean that the llama is alert. Ears raised or bent slightly forward seems to mean the llama is feeling happy.

Llamas that are raised as pets are very gentle and loving animals. They are also great with children. But females make better pets than males because males tend to be more aggressive.

Llamas are very intelligent animals and can be trained easily. You can train a llama to walk on a leash, the way you would walk a dog. A llama can learn how to lie down on command. One owner said that her pet llama learned how to drink iced tea from a cup and would also nuzzle in her ear if she asked it to "tell me a secret." A llama can easily become a part of your family during its long life span of up to 20 years.

Llamas are easier to care for than a number of other animals. Unlike horses, llamas are comfortable when kept in smaller spaces. Four llamas can stay on an acre of land, and even a large backyard would do for one. Llamas are also much cheaper to feed. They come from desert regions where food is hard to find. So their ancestors learned to survive on smaller amounts of food than sheep and

A Guard Llama?

Both male and female llamas make very good guards. Ranchers in the United States use llamas to guard flocks of sheep. They have also been used to guard geese, ducks, deer, and cattle. Llamas are aggressive toward predators, such as wolves, foxes, coyotes, and domestic dogs. When danger approaches, they give an alarm call as a warning to the flock. The llama may try to chase the predator away or kick it with its hind legs. Llamas can be very strong and forceful and can kill predators that threaten their flock.

The Llama's Little Cousin

The alpaca is a smaller version of the llama, standing 3 to 4 feet (0.9 to 1.2 meters) at the head and weighing 100 to 170 pounds (45 to 77 kilograms). Like llamas, alpacas are very gentle animals, and their smaller size makes them very desirable pets, although they have been slower to become popular in North America than llamas.

Alpacas are too small to haul heavy loads, but they have long been prized for their high-quality wool. Alpaca wool is longer, lighter, softer, stronger, and warmer than llama wool. In fact, alpaca wool was a sign of wealth among the ancient Incas. The royal family wore alpaca robes. Today, alpacas cost much more to buy than llamas, mainly because their wool is so valuable.

other livestock animals need. Llamas can handle all kinds of weather. But they have more problems with the heat than the cold, so they need to have plenty of water and a shady area during the summer. You can put your llama in a wading pool or have a fan blowing on it to keep it from getting overheated. A barn is a good shelter to protect llamas from extreme hot and cold weather.

Llamas are environment-friendly. While horses, cows, and sheep can chop up the ground with their cutting hooves, llamas have soft, leathery pads on the bottom of their feet, so they won't ruin your backyard. They clean their coats in a "dust bath," kicking up dust as they roll on the ground. Llamas will deposit a few piles of dung in the yard, leaving the rest of the land clean.

INTERNET RESOURCES

Llamas:

http://www.eskimo.com/~wallama.faq.htm "Frequently Asked Questions and some strange answers"

http://www.llamapaedia.com/ "Llamapaedia" (articles on history, behavior, and llama raising)

http://www.webcom/~degraham/welcome.html "Llama Web" (information, fun and games, events, and links to llama farms and services)

wysiwyg://168/http://www.llamaweb.com/About/ "About Llamas" by Dale Graham (information on camelids, llama raising)

Alpacas:

http://www.alpacanet.com/history.html "Alpacas: A Brief History from South America to Current American Herd Status"

http://www.ctalpacas.com/facts.htm "Alpaca Facts"

http://www.pacaweb.com/alpaca.html "The Alpaca," Alpaca Owners and Breeders Association

FAST FACTS

Scientific name	*Equus caballus* in Family Equidae. The donkey is *Equus asinus*.
Cost	Ranges from hundreds to tens of thousands of dollars
Food	Grass, hay, grain, oats
Housing	Fenced-in grassy area (backyard size is fine); barn or other type of shelter, such as an 8-by-10-foot (2.5-by-3-meter) shed, should be available
Training	Always be gentle when training to the halter.
Special notes	You may need a permit to keep "farm animals."

MINIATURE HORSE

MINIATURE HORSE AND DONKEY

HOW MANY TIMES HAVE you tried to convince your parents to buy you a horse? Horses are beautiful animals. But owning a horse is a large responsibility—it requires a great deal of food, living space, time, and money.

Having a horse as a pet might seem a little overwhelming. But what if you had a horse about the size of a dog? The miniature horse—a small version of the regular-size horse—is becoming popular as a pet. Miniature horses are not only small, they are very gentle and affectionate—the perfect pet for children. However, though these animals are miniature, their prices are not.

BREEDING FOR SIZE

Miniature horses have been around since the 1500s. They were specially bred as pets for the royal families of Europe. Miniature horses were so much easier to manage and were great companions for young princes and princesses. These small horses were also used in England and northern Europe as work animals to pull ore carts in coal mines. They could also go to other places that were too small for big horses.

By the late 1800s, some miniature horses were brought to the United States after the breed became fairly well established. These horses were used to pull carts in the mines of West Virginia, Indiana, and Ohio as recently as the 1950s. Now, however, miniature horses are used more for play than for work. Years and years of selective breeding have created the fine stock of miniature horses we have today.

MINIATURE HORSE PETS

The miniature horse stands no more than 34 inches (86 centimeters) tall at the shoulders, and the adult weighs an average of 150 pounds (60 kilograms). That is a huge difference from its 6- to 7-foot (183- to 213-centimeter) cousin that weighs more than 1000 pounds (454 kilograms). Miniature horses are not ponies, dwarfs, or runts. They do not have a genetic disorder. Miniature horses are simply smaller versions of their taller relatives. They still look like quarter horses, Arabians, Thoroughbreds, and draft horses. Like all horses, miniature horses come in a variety of colors—black, bay, chestnut, brown, sorrel, roan, buckskin,

The Falabella Breed

During the mid-1800s, the Falabella family of Argentina wanted to produce a breed of horse that was the size of a pony but had the characteristics and personality of a horse and could be handled by children and adults. Careful selective breeding produced a new breed of horse that became known as the Falabella.

The Falabella's bloodlines can be traced back to the 1500s when the Spanish conquistadores brought Andalusian horses to Latin America. These animals were set free to reproduce in the wild. The harsh conditions made the horses very sturdy. The Falabella family carefully crossbred descendants of these "wild" horses with small Thoroughbreds, Welsh ponies, and Shetland ponies to produce today's small, sturdy, yet attractive Falabella horses.

Unlike some other miniature horses, this breed consistently produces offspring with a small size and typical temperament and appearance. Falabella horses can live for 40 years or more.

palomino, gray, silver, and white. They may be a solid color, a mixture of colors, or an Appaloosa.

Horses are sociable; they seem happiest in the company of other animals. Miniature horses also like being with people. They like to be handled and thrive on attention. In fact, some pet owners say that miniature horses are more gentle and affectionate than some of the larger breeds.

Miniature horses are very smart animals. They can easily be trained to a halter and lead. They can also learn to pull carts like their ancestors. They can pull a tremendous amount of weight in a cart—about 300 to 400 pounds (136 to 181 kilograms)—for several hours.

Miniature horses need little room and small amounts of food compared to regular-size horses. A miniature horse would be happy in a person's backyard, with a shed for shelter, and as little as a tenth of the food that larger horses eat. (Some people keep their pet miniature horses indoors and say they can be housebroken, like a dog that "asks" to go out.)

A miniature horse can give you years of enjoyment in its long lifespan of 20 to 30 years or more.

DID YOU KNOW?
Miniature horses can jump much higher, in proportion to their body size, than regular-size horses. A large horse would have to jump 7 feet (more than 2 meters) to match what a miniature horse can do.

INTERNET RESOURCES

Horses:

http://expage.com/page/magicmam "Amazing World of Miniature Horses"

http://www.ansi.okstate.edu/breeds/horses/falabell/ "Breeds of Livestock—Falabella Horses" (information and photos)

Miniature Donkeys

The donkey was the first member of the horse family to be domesticated, more than 4,500 years ago. The first miniature donkeys were brought to the United States in 1929 from the Mediterranean islands of Sicily and Sardinia. Like miniature horses, miniature donkeys are becoming popular pets.

Unlike miniature horses, miniature donkeys have not been bred down from larger ancestors. The ancestors of these donkeys were between 32 and 38 inches (81 to 96 centimeters) tall. By selecting the smallest animals, breeders produced today's miniatures, whose height is between 31 and 35 inches (79 to 89 centimeters). Their average weight is 200 to 450 pounds (91 to 204 kilograms).

Donkeys are famous for being stubborn. They may just plant their feet into the ground and refuse to move. It is not clear why they do this. The animal may be tired or cautious about what is ahead. On the other hand, it may just be trying to get its own way. Though it may be difficult to get the donkey to go where you want it to go, it can be halter-trained and will learn to follow you.

Many pet owners say that miniature donkeys are very gentle and affectionate animals that seem to love attention. Donkeys do not need much room—you can fit ten donkeys on one acre of land. Miniature donkeys are hardy animals and have been known to live more than 40 years!

http://www.ansi.okstate.edu/breeds/horses/miniatur/ "Breeds of Livestock—Miniature Horses"

http://www.falabellamini.com/ "Falabella—The Original Miniature Horse" (photos, history, and horses for sale at Rabbit Run Miniature Horses)

http://www.iinet.com/users/lvrvvk/lvrhorse.html "What Can Miniature Horses Do?"

http://www2.littlehorses.com/horses/breeds.htm "Falabella Breed Information Page" (history, characteristics, and care)

Donkeys:

http://planetpets.simplenet.com/donkey.htm "Miniature Donkeys"

http://www.oregontrail.net/~bmorgan/the facts.htm "Miniature Donkey Facts"

http://www.orenet.org/~jrachau/ "The Donkey Page" (background, care, and links to donkey breeders and clubs)

http://www.qis.net/~minidonk/donktext.htm "Miniature Donkeys. . .All You Need To Know About Donkeys!" by Miniature Donkey Talk Magazine and the International Miniature Donkey Registry (information and photos)

http://www.valleystables-exotics.com/donkeys.htm "Miniature Sicilian Donkeys" (information and photos)

FAST FACTS

Scientific name	Bush baby: *Galago* in Family Lorisidae, Order Primates Capuchin: *Cebus* in Family Cebidae, Order Primates Marmoset: *Hapala, Saguinus, and Calithrax* in Family Callitridicae, Order Primates Rhesus monkey: *Macaca mulatta* in Family Cercopithecidae, Order Primates Spider monkey: *Ateles* in Family Cebidae, Order Primates Woolly monkey: *Lagothrix lagotricha* in Family Cebidae, Order Primates
Cost	About $500 to $5000
Food	Monkey pellets, canned primate diet with supplements of vegetables, fruit, meat, eggs, etc. depending on species
Housing	If caged, need plenty of space; warm, humid conditions; if allowed free run of the house, lock up medicines and other dangerous things
Training	Very smart; can learn tricks but cannot be housebroken; require frequent gentle but firm handling from an early age
Special notes	Permits necessary and may have to be renewed each year; some places do not permit keeping monkeys because of health hazards; not good pets for children.

CAPUCHIN
MONKEY

MONKEYS

PEOPLE LOVE TO WATCH the monkeys at the zoo. They look so much like little humans, and they seem full of fun as they chatter, make faces, swing from one place to another, throw things, and peel bananas with their clever, humanlike hands. They might seem like ideal pets—fun-loving friends.

Monkeys really *are* a lot like people. Along with the larger apes, they are our closest relatives in the animal kingdom. They are smart and playful and can be fascinating companions. But they are also very complex creatures. Like people, they can get bored and mischievous, lose their tempers, sulk, and carry grudges. A young monkey is sweet and lovable but also demanding, messy, and often destructive; when it gets older, it may become dangerous. Having a pet monkey is a big responsibility—more than most people can handle.

> **DID YOU KNOW?**
> The word *monkey* comes from a Latin word, *homunculus*, which means "little man."

BRANCHES ON OUR FAMILY TREE

Scientists believe that both humans and monkeys are descended from little tree shrews that lived about 65 million years ago. These were the first primates, the order to which we belong. Life among the treetops was rewarding for clever, agile animals with big eyes to judge distances, nimble hands to catch insects and grasp hold of tree branches, and a good sense of balance.

As time went by, the first primates spread out and developed into a variety of monkeys. Some had long tails that helped them balance as they scampered through the trees; others had no tails at all. The New World monkeys that lived in the tropics of South America developed long, grasping tails that could wrap around a branch and cling firmly, almost like an extra hand. The Old World monkeys in Asia and Africa did not have grasping tails. Larger apes split off from this branch of our family tree and produced the present-day chimpanzees, gorillas, gibbons, and orangutans, as well as the apelike creatures that were our ancestors.

A number of monkey species have been kept as pets. Marmosets and tamarins are small, colorful South American monkeys with long, silky hair and long tails.

Capuchins were named for the crests of stiff hair on their heads, which look like the hoods worn by Capuchin monks (members of a religious order). Spider monkeys swing through the trees with their long arms and legs. Dangling from a branch by its long, grasping tail, this monkey does look rather like a big spider. Woolly monkeys are larger than most New World monkeys, weighing up to 20 pounds (9 kilograms) when full-grown. They look very humanlike, with dark, hairless faces, hands, and feet. Rhesus monkeys and other macaques are the only Old World monkeys that have been kept as pets. They are also used for laboratory experiments because they are so similar to humans.

> ### Apes That Speak
>
> *Large primates, such as gorillas, chimpanzees, and bonobos (pygmy chimpanzees), have been raised by scientists who wished to study their behavior and intelligence. The structure of an ape's mouth and throat does not allow it to produce all the sounds of human speech, but some apes have learned to communicate with humans using sign language. A bonobo named Kanzi learned to "speak" by pressing keys for symbols on a computer keyboard while sitting on his mother's lap as researchers tried to teach the mother.*

MONKEYS AS PETS

Having a pet monkey can be like raising a toddler—it is lively, active, and hard to control. As the monkey gets older, it grows smarter and stronger, but it cannot be toilet trained (millions of years of living in trees produced habits of letting the droppings fall where they may), and its behavior is like a child at the "terrible twos" stage. If given free run of the house, it can quickly open cabinets and trash their contents, rip screens, open locked doors, and—if it is annoyed in some way—bite people. Monkeys tend to get more aggressive as they grow to adulthood.

But many pet monkeys do not live to be adults. The warm, humid conditions of their tropical homelands are very hard to produce in a house in which people also live, and some owners keep their monkeys in cages that are too small for them to get enough exercise. Because pet monkeys look and act like little people, some inexperienced owners feed their monkeys table scraps of "people food," and the pets do not get the nourishment they need. Monkeys can also catch illnesses from people (and they may carry diseases, such as tuberculosis, that they can transmit to humans). Sadly, although some monkeys live for 20 to 40 years or more, most pet monkeys die after only a year or two.

INTERNET RESOURCES

http://members.primary.net/~heather/articles/care.html "General Monkey Ownership Info.," reprint of a 1975 article by Madeline Darrow

http://www.cdmnet.com/heather "Heather's Wild World of Animals: The Best Pet Monkey Site on the Net!" (information, photos; FAQ by Heather Bretz; "Are You Sure You Want a Monkey" available by e-mail)

http://www.intournet.net/exotic/info1.html "Monkeys as House Apes" by Dori English (including "The Six Most Common Reasons People Buy Pet Monkeys" and "The 12 Most Common Reasons People Give Up Pet Monkeys")

http://www.intournet.net/exotic/info2.html "Monkeys as House Apes" by Dori English

F A S T   F A C T S

Scientific name	*Sus scrofa domestica* in Family Suidae (Old World Pigs)
Cost	Registered potbellies about $200-$500; cheaper (maybe less reliable) from private owners; free from animal shelters
Food	Pig pellets, dog food, table scraps; use nontip water bowl
Housing	A safe room indoors and an outdoor pen with a doghouse and a shady area are best; a child's wading pool for wallowing
Training	Use positive rewards (not punishment) to teach tricks and housebreak (pigs naturally use a single "toilet area").
Special notes	Some places may not permit keeping "farm animals."

POTBELLIED PIG

POTBELLIED PIG

MOST PEOPLE THINK OF pigs as big, messy, lazy, greedy, and generally piggish. But thousands of potbellied pig owners would dispute that. They say their pets are smart, cute, cuddly, and clean.

NOT REALLY PIGGISH

Even full-sized farm pigs don't really deserve their reputation. They roll in mud because the wet mud helps them to keep cool. If a pool of water is available, they'll wallow in that, instead. Pigs on a farm are kept in pens and fed more food than they really need to make them gain weight quickly. But pigs living wild get plenty of exercise and eat just the right amounts of food to keep themselves trim and healthy. Pigs are also very smart—more intelligent than dogs, cats, and most other animals.

The pigs raised on farms in the United States are big, though. Most hogs (full-grown pigs) weigh 300 to 500 pounds (136 to 227 kilograms). Imaging snuggling up to a pet like that! Fortunately, there are small breeds that make good pets.

> **DID YOU KNOW?**
> Winston Churchill once said, "I like pigs. Dogs look up to us. Cats look down on us. Pigs treat us as equals."

PIGS FOR PETS

The ancestors of today's popular miniature pigs lived wild in China. By the tenth century, they had been domesticated and were raised as pets and food animals all over Southeast Asia. In the mid-twentieth century, Vietnamese potbellied pigs were imported to Europe, and then to Canada. They first reached the United States in 1985.

Full-grown potbellied pigs weigh an average of about 60 pounds (27 kilograms). Short and stubby—about 12 to 16 inches (30 to 41 centimeters) tall—they have a round potbelly that gives them their name. These little pigs were originally jet black, but now some of them have spots of white or tan. Potbellied pigs' short, wrinkled, pushed-in noses are smaller than most hog snouts. Their ears stand up straight, and they have a straight tail that wags like a dog's tail. They make little grunts and honking sounds, bark to warn of danger, and squeal when excited or hurt.

Pigs are naturally sociable. In the wild, they live in groups and sleep snuggled up together. Potbellies are just as sociable, and when raised as pets, they are affectionate with people. They are naturally clean animals and are easy to housebreak. They can learn to use a litter box or pace back and forth by the door when they need to go outside. Another plus: potbellied pigs don't shed, and their hair is free of dander (flaky bits of skin that cause allergies).

Like their larger relatives, these little pigs are quite intelligent. You can teach them to come when they are called, sit up and beg, roll over, dance, climb stairs, and catch a Frisbee. With a harness and leash you can take a pet potbelly for a walk. It will snuggle up and watch TV with you or keep you company while you read. This is a pet that will stay around for a long time, too, with a lifespan of about 20 years.

Most pet shops do not sell miniature pigs because many states have restrictions against selling farm animals in stores, but they can be obtained from specialized breeders in various parts of the country. A registered pig costs more, but you know what its parents looked like and can be surer that it will not grow a lot bigger than you expected.

> ## Problem Pigs
>
> *You have to be firm with a pet potbelly from the beginning, or it will quickly turn into a spoiled pig that demands constant attention and tries to boss the family around. This can get scary when it grows up. Pigs also like to "root" for food and will dig up the yard (or your carpet) if they do not have a pile of hay or old blankets to root in. Inexpensive "toys" such as plastic buckets and jugs, cardboard boxes, and burlap sacks help keep them from getting bored and mischievous when you are out. Pigs sunburn easily, so outdoor play or living areas should include shady spots.*

INTERNET RESOURCES

http://www.potbellypigs.com The North American Potbellied Pig Association pages, including helpful information and contacts to breeders

http://www.sieranet.net/ National Committees on Potbellied Pigs pages

FAST FACTS

Scientific name	*Capras hircus* in Family Bovidae
Cost	Males cost about $75, females about $100
Food	Grass, grain, hay, oats, brush and dry leaves
Housing	Grassy area, with fence at least 4 feet (1.2 meters) high; backyard is fine. Include something to climb on or balance on. Also, a barn or other type of shelter, such as an 8-by-10-foot (2.5-by-3-meter) shed, should be available to protect against extreme temperatures.
Training	Use positive rewards (not punishment) to "housebreak," and to train to follow on command, or obey other gestures; can use treats, such as whole kernel corn, for training.
Special notes	You may need a permit to keep "farm animals."

PYGMY GOATS

PYGMY GOAT

WOULDN'T IT BE NICE to have a sweet and gentle pet that helps around the house, too? If you owned a pygmy goat, this pet could help to mow your lawn. Pygmy goats love to feed on grass, which makes for a nice, trim lawn.

Pet owners say that pygmy goats make great pets because they are small and take up little room; they are inexpensive to buy and feed; and they are very affectionate animals. But watch out—goats are curious animals and can be very mischievous.

COMING TO AMERICA

The pygmy goat used to be called the Cameroon Dwarf Goat because it originated in the Cameroon area of West Africa. Some of these small goats were sent from Africa to zoos in Europe, and later to Canada. The first pygmy goats in the United States for which proper records have been kept arrived from Sweden in 1959. Breeders sold the animals to zoos, medical researchers, and individuals. Since then, pygmy goats have been growing more and more popular.

PYGMY GOAT PETS

The pygmy goat, as its name suggests, is a small goat—about one third the size of a regular-size goat. An adult pygmy goat stands between 16 and 23 inches (40 to 58 centimeters) at the shoulders and weighs about 40 to 70 pounds (18 to 32 kilograms). Its legs are short in proportion to its body, unlike another miniature goat breed, the Nigerian dwarf goat. (Despite its name, the Nigerian dwarf goat is a midget rather than a true dwarf, with body and legs in the same proportions as a full-size goat.) Pygmy goats come in a variety of colors: white, black, brown, silver grey, as well as combinations of these colors. Male goats have beards. Females may not have a beard, or it may be trimmed. Like other goats, pygmy goats communicate with bleating sounds.

Pygmy goats are very hardy animals. They can handle different types of weather, even very cold temperatures. But they do not like dampness or wind.

> **DID YOU KNOW?**
> Goats are closely related to sheep. There are some major differences between the two animals, though. Goats, for instance, are much smarter and friendlier than sheep.

39

Goats that Faint?

Fainting goats do not actually faint. They have a hereditary disorder that causes their muscles to lock when they are surprised or scared. This is something like the defensive behavior of opossums and spiders, which may "play dead" when they are in danger. Sometimes the goat falls over. You are more likely to see a younger goat "faint" than an older one because older goats have learned to compensate by spending a lot of time leaning against a fence or barn.

Fainting goats were first recognized in the 1880s in Marshall County, Tennessee. They are small goats but not miniatures and were used to protect sheep from predators. If coyotes or dogs attacked the flock, the goats "fainted" and the sheep could run away. The goats were often eaten by the predators, though, and by the 1980s the fainting goat was close to extinction. Today, they are no longer endangered. People who keep them as pets say that fainting goats are very calm, sweet-natured animals.

Pygmy goats are sociable animals. They get along well with other goats, sheep, or even horses. These little goats are more gentle and affectionate than their taller relatives, which makes them much more suitable as pets. As with all animals, pygmy goats that are raised as pets from a young age make the best companions.

Pygmy goats are active animals and can be very interesting to watch as they jump and dance around in the pasture or backyard. One pet owner claimed that her pygmy goats would hop on their hind legs. She also said that her goats often climbed trees!

DID YOU KNOW?
Many people enjoy milking their pet pygmy goats. Goat's milk is much easier to digest and contains less fat than cow's milk.

Like all goats, they also love to chew on things. This is not a problem when they trim your grass, but it can be very frustrating when they start munching on bushes and hedges. Trees in the yard must also be protected, because the goat would eat the bark, killing the tree.

Pygmy goats can be rather naughty at times. A certain pet owner said that her pygmy goat was having a little too much fun; it was jumping on the roof of the family car! They can also unhook latches and jump or climb over fences.

Pygmy goats are very smart animals and can be trained to do many things. Your pet pygmy goat can learn to come when you call it by name. It can also be trained to walk on a leash and follow you around on its own. It may also be housebroken. One pet owner said that her pygmy goat learned how to "cry" at the door like a little dog until she would let it out.

Female pygmy goats make better pets than males. Males are more aggressive than females and they give off an odor, especially around mating time.

INTERNET RESOURCES

http://goatweb.com/dwarfs.html "Nigerian Dwarf Goats" by the Nigerian Dwarf Goat Association and American Goat Society (background information, breed standards, and pictures)

http://goatweb.com/pygmies.html "African Pygmy goats" by the National Pygmy Goat Association and American Goat Society (breed standards, pictures)

http://home.rmci.net/weltonsfancy/Goats.htm "General Care and Information for Fainting Goats and Pygmy Goats"

http://planetpets.simplenet.com/goat.htm "Nigerian Dwarf Goat" (information provided by Brenda Rivoire and the Irvine Mesa Charros 4-H Club; but the picture shown is an African pygmy goat)

http://www.cvm.uiuc.edu/ceps/petcolumns/Pygmy.htm "Pygmy Goats Can Be Fun Backyard Pets," by Kimberly Meenen of University of Illinois College of Veterinary Medicine (pet column for January 15, 1996)

http://www.webworksltd.com/webpub/Goats/Faintinggoat.html "American Tennessee Fainting Goat Association" (background and information on Fainting goats)

FAST FACTS

Scientific name	*Petaurus breviceps* in Family Petauridae, Order Diprotodontia
Cost	Babies to age 2: $125; ages 3 to 9: $100; age 10+: $75 Breeding pairs: $150/pair
Food	Picky eaters, but will eat a wide variety of foods including fruits, berries, vegetables, bread, nuts, cooked egg, insects (mealworms, crickets), meats (turkey and chicken parts), and special glider supplement. Food and water should be located near the top of the cage.
Housing	A large, tall wire cage at least 20-by-20-by-36 inches (51-by-51-by-91 centimeters). Must include a tree branch for climbing and a nesting box or cloth pouch located near the top of the cage.
Training	Use treats for training. Be gentle and use positive reinforcements, especially while bonding with the glider.
Special notes	It may be illegal to own a sugar glider in some areas, or a permit may be needed.

SUGAR GLIDER

SUGAR GLIDER

HOW WOULD YOU LIKE A pet that can take a nap in your shirt pocket while you are washing the dishes or surfing the Net? Sugar gliders are adorable pocket pets that seem to love to be close to their owners. These affectionate animals can make interesting pets, but a sugar glider needs two very important things to live a happy and healthy life: plenty of attention and lots of room so it can do what it does best—glide through the air.

A LIVING KITE

Sugar gliders got their name because they love sweet foods and because of their remarkable ability to glide through the air. In the wild, these animals spend most of the time in trees. In fact, they can go through their whole lives without ever being on the ground thanks to an amazing adaptation that helps them go from one tree to the next. Sugar gliders have furry flaps of skin that extend from their wrists to their ankles. When a sugar glider leaps off a tall branch, it glides through the air, looking just like a kite. It uses its long tail to steer. The sugar glider may also use the winds to travel up to 150 feet (46 meters) in a single glide! It comes in to a smooth landing, with its feet planted firmly on the tree branch.

A UNIQUE SPECIES

Sugar gliders are small marsupials that can be found in the treetops of Australia, Indonesia, New Guinea, and New Zealand. Like other marsupials, the female keeps her young in a pouch on her belly.

Australia is home to many unique creatures. In fact, some species native to Australia are not like any other animals in the rest of the world. That's because the mammals on that continent evolved separately from those elsewhere after Australia broke off from the rest of the continents millions of years ago. Nearly all the marsupials in the rest of the world were replaced by mammals that nourished their babies before birth through an organ called the placenta, which allowed them to develop more completely. That is why you would not be able to find koalas, kangaroos, sugar gliders, or other Australian mammals anywhere else in the world.

Sugar gliders are quickly becoming popular pets in the United States. Australia stopped exporting these unique creatures many years ago. The sugar gliders presently in the United States are descendants of gliders that were imported from other places, primarily Indonesia.

SUGAR GLIDER PETS

A sugar glider has a gray coat with a cream color underside. A black stripe runs from the animal's nose down the back of its body and to the end of its black tail. Another black stripe outlines the eyes and runs back to its large, sensitive ears. A sugar glider's body is about 5 to 6 inches (12.7 to 15.2 centimeters) long with a tail of about equal length. Adult males weigh about 4 to 5.5 ounces (114 to 160 grams), while females weigh a little less, around 3.35 to 4.8 ounces (95 to 135 grams). Sugar gliders use various sounds to communicate. They make noises such as "crabbing," a kind of screeching sound, when they are frightened or annoyed. You may hear this sound when you first take home your sugar glider pet. They may also make ticking sounds, similar to the sound that you make with your tongue, to show that they are annoyed. Sugar gliders may bark like a puppy to get attention. Chirping or muttering is a sign of a happy glider.

> ### Similar Strangers
>
> *Sugar gliders look very similar to flying squirrels. Like sugar gliders, flying squirrels have a folded skin that extends so that it can glide (not fly) through the air. Although these two animals have similar adaptations, they are not related to one another.*

Sugar gliders are very social animals. In the wild, they live in groups of six to fifteen or more gliders. This need for companionship makes it easy for sugar gliders to bond with people. If you want to raise a happy, healthy sugar glider, spend at least two hours each day playing with your pet. Some glider pet owners say that sugar gliders are happiest when they have a friend. So buying two gliders may be a good idea.

Sugar gliders are very active animals. They need a lot of room to play, especially since they like to glide through the air. Their cage should be very large—the bigger the better. The cage should also have a tree branch for climbing. Sugar gliders are very good climbers, so you need to keep an eye on them because they can get into a lot of trouble.

Sugar gliders are clean animals. However, they do have scent glands located in three different areas: on the head, on the chest, and near the rear. A sugar glider may rub its head on you to mark you as part of its territory. It is something like a handshake to say "Hi, how are you?" In the wild, this scent is a way for sugar gliders to identify themselves to other gliders. Fortunately, a sugar glider's scent is not nearly as smelly as a ferret's or a skunk's, but it can be rather annoying.

Sugar gliders can be trained to do certain things with the help of treats.

Give your sugar glider a treat to teach it to stay in your pocket during the day. (Gliders sleep during the day so chances are it may sleep in your pocket all day.) Gliders can also be trained to glide from a high object in the room and land right on your shoulder. They cannot be trained to use a litter box, however. For easy cleaning, a tray should be kept underneath your pet's large wire cage.

With a lifespan up to 15 years, sugar gliders require a long commitment. But a tame glider will give its owner lots of love and devotion in return.

INTERNET RESOURCES

http://members.aol.com/hkeane/webdoc5.htm "About Sugar Gliders" by Heather Paul-Keane (lots of pet care information)

http://www.angelfire.com/tx/facehugger/info.html "Information on Sugar Gliders" with links to audio files of sugar glider sounds, sugar glider FAQ, and sugar glider video

http://www.animalnetwork.com/critters/profiles/sugarglider/default.asp "Animal Network's Critter Collection: Sugar Gliders: Personality Plus Attitude" by Pat Storer (background, pet care, and tips)

http://www.intournet.net/exotic/glidercare.html "ISGA Sugar Glider Caresheet" by the International Sugar Glider Association (background, pet care, nutrition, and training)

http://www.pygmypets.com/ "Pygmy Pets: Sugar Gliders" by Caroline MacPherson (information and pictures on what sugar gliders are like as pets, care instructions, nutrition questions, and related species)

NOT A PET!

READING ABOUT THE unusual animals described in this book has probably left you with some important thoughts:

- Most of them would be better off left in the wild

- Keeping any of them as a pet is challenging and demanding

- With a very few exceptions, they are not good choices as pets for children

Besides many of the animals in this book, there are some other very exotic and appealing animals that probably should not be pets for almost anyone, for a variety of reasons. Some people have kept pet ocelots, for example. These beautiful spotted cats can be tamed and make elegant and affectionate pets. But, except for a few specially licensed breeders in zoos and private collections, it is illegal to buy or keep them. Ocelots, and a number of other wild cat species, are endangered in their native habitats. Taking young animals from the wild to be raised in captivity can upset the balance of nature in their home and make it more difficult for their species to survive.

It is also illegal to capture and keep our native wildlife species, even if they are not endangered. It might be a big temptation to try to tame and raise a baby chipmunk that you found, or an adorable little fawn that seems to be wandering around lost in the woods. But that is a temptation you should resist. A fawn that seems to be an orphan, for example, usually has a mother hiding nearby, and it needs her milk to give it the right nourishment and protection against diseases.

That cute little animal you found might also hurt you. If it is frightened, it may bite you—and some animals may be carrying diseases such as rabies, or parasites like the ticks that carry Lyme disease or Rocky Mountain spotted fever.

If you find a wild animal that seems to be lost or hurt, the best thing to do is to contact the nearest office of your state's Division of Fish, Game, and Wildlife. It will contact a licensed rehabilitator who will be able to give the animal the care it needs.

FOR FURTHER INFORMATION

Note: Before attempting to keep a kind of pet that is new to you, it is a good idea to read one or more pet manuals about that species. Check your local library, pet shop, or bookstore. Search for information on the species on the Internet.

BOOKS

Burn, Barbara. *A Practical Guide to Impractical Pets.* NY: Howell Book House, 1997.

Chrystie, Frances N., and Margery Facklam. *Pets: A Comprehensive Handbook for Kids,* Revised edition. Boston: Little, Brown, 1995.

Messonnier, Shawn. *Exotic Pets: A Veterinary Guide for Owners.* Plano, TX: Wordware Publishing, 1995.

Siino, Betsy Sikora. *You Want WHAT for a Pet?!* NY: Howell Book House, 1996.

INTERNET RESOURCES

http://www.animalsforsale.com/exotic.htm "The Joy and the Commitment" by Pat Storer (things to consider about owning exotic pets)

http://www.nwlink.com/~pawprint/petparts_b4ubuy.html "Before You Buy" (things to consider before getting a pet)

http://www.nwlink.com/~pawprint/petparts_exotic.html "The Exotic Factor" (special needs and responsibilities for exotic pets)

http://www.nwlink.com/~pawprint/petparts_kids.html "Kids & Kritters" (questions to decide about pets for children)

INDEX

Page numbers in *italics* refer to illustrations.